Which dinosaurs carried clubs?

Dinosaurs
and Prehistoric Animals

ISBN 0-87197-487-8

Produced by Miles Kelly Publishing Ltd
Bardfield Centre, Great Bardfield, Essex CM7 4SL, UK

Editorial Director: Anne Marshall
Editor: Mark Darling
Copy Editor and Indexer: Lynn Bresler
Proofreader: Margaret Berrill
Senior Designer: Jo Brewer
Designers: Sally Lace, Debbie Meekcoms, Robert Walster
Artwork Commissioning: Lesley Cartlidge
Picture Research: Ruth Boardman, Jennifer Hunt, Liberty Newton
Art Director: Clare Sleven

Color reproduction: DPI Colour, Saffron Walden, Essex, UK

Printed in China

CEO: Ralph Mosley
President: Jerry Heffel
Sales Directors: Fred Prevost, Creig Soeder, Dave Causer,
Roy Loftin, Jeff Hawley

Vice President, Marketing: Dan Moore
Project Director: Fiona Greenland
Editorial Director: Mary Cummings
Copy Editor: Carolyn King
Associate Editor: Lisa Fairfax
Production Director: Mark Sloan
Production Coordinator: Powell Ropp
Production Manager: Tom Norvell

Specialist Consultants: Dr Belinda Ashon, Clive Carpenter, Janet Dyson MEd (education consultant), Dr Jim Flegg OBE,
Tim Furniss, Steve Parker BSc (Scientific Fellow of the Zoological Society of London), Peter Riley BSc, Cbiol, MIBiol, PGCE,
Richard Tames MA MSc
Authors: Anita Ganeri MA (Fellow of the Royal Geographical Society), Neil Morris BA, Clare Oliver, Chris Oxlade BSc,
Steve Parker BSc, Philip Steele BA, Brenda Williams
The publishers would also like to thank: Cindy Leaney MA, DTEFLA, CTEFLA

The publishers would like to thank the following artists whose work appears in this book: Mark Davis, Peter Dennis,
Richard Draper, Chris Forsey, Mike Foster/Maltings Partnership, Tony Kenyon, Sue King/SGA, Kevin Maddison,
Debbie Meekcoms, Jane Pickering, Terry Riley, Steve Roberts, Mike Saunders, Rudi Vizi, Paul Williams.

Contents

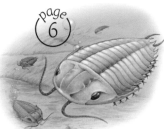

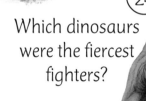
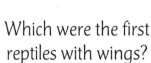

3

Why have some forms of life disappeared?

If you were to travel back in time, you would see different animals and forms of life. Some forms of these animals and plants are still around today, but many lived only in the past. No one is sure why some animals disappeared. Perhaps they were hunted by other animals. Some may have disappeared because it became too hot or too cold. Perhaps a meteor or comet hit the Earth or a great flood destroyed them. No one knows for sure.

Rhamphorhynchus

Spinosaurus

On land

Moschops

👆 **Jet-propelled shells**

In ancient seas, ammonites moved like jet aircraft do today — but they shot backward when they squirted out jets of water.

Which fish swam on mountaintops?

Over a very long time, the Earth has changed. Places that were once under the ocean are now land. That is why prehistoric fish remains can be found on mountaintops.

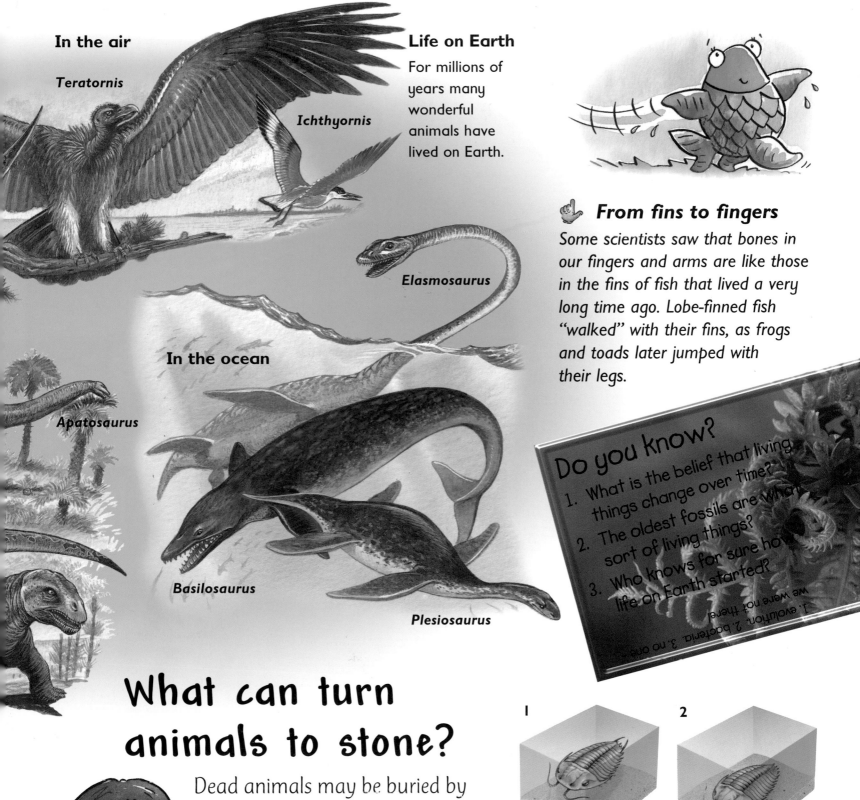

In the air

Teratornis

Ichthyornis

Life on Earth

For millions of years many wonderful animals have lived on Earth.

Elasmosaurus

In the ocean

Apatosaurus

Basilosaurus

Plesiosaurus

From fins to fingers

Some scientists saw that bones in our fingers and arms are like those in the fins of fish that lived a very long time ago. Lobe-finned fish "walked" with their fins, as frogs and toads later jumped with their legs.

Do you know?

1. What is the belief that living things change over time?
2. The oldest fossils are what sort of living things?
3. Who knows for sure how life on Earth started?

1. evolution 2. bacteria 3. no one — we were not there!

What can turn animals to stone?

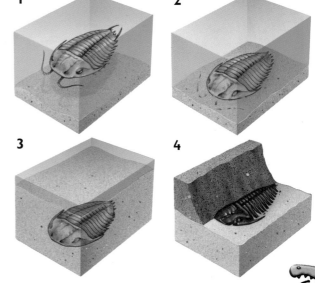

Dead animals may be buried by mud or sand that later turns hard. Over time, the hard mud is pressed down and turns into rock, trapping what is left of the animal inside. The animal remains also turn to stone, and they are called fossils.

1

2

3

4

Which was the first animal to have eyes?

Trilobites looked a bit like woodlice, but they swam, crawled, and ran on the sea bed a very long time ago. Their bodies had lots of segments and legs, and as the trilobite grew, it threw off its old shell for a bigger one. Old shells often became fossils, and these tell us that trilobites were the first animals with eyes. Their big, curved eyes could see above, behind, in front, and sideways all at the same time!

Which ancient animal can you squeeze in the bathtub?

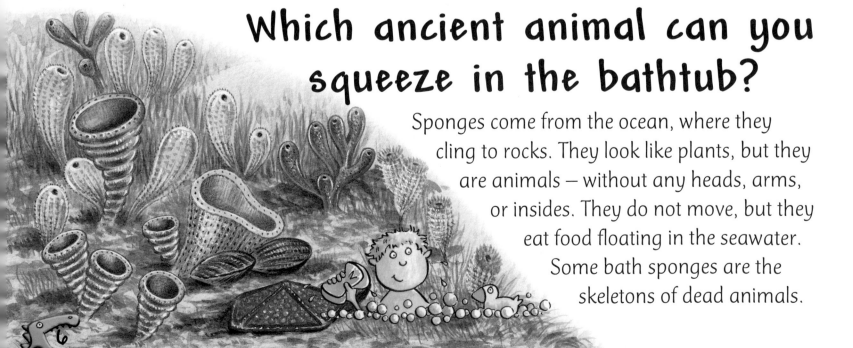

Sponges come from the ocean, where they cling to rocks. They look like plants, but they are animals – without any heads, arms, or insides. They do not move, but they eat food floating in the seawater. Some bath sponges are the skeletons of dead animals.

What animals might you find in chalk?

Chalk cliffs are mostly made of the tiny shells and skeletons of ancient sea animals. Large parts of the Earth that were under the ocean a long time ago are now land. The sea bed got harder and harder and turned into rock, with the remains of the animals trapped inside it. The chalk we use for writing and drawing is quite similar and is also called chalk.

Inside out

Skeletons gave animals a fixed shape. Worn outside as a shell, they made animals like trilobites safer from attack.

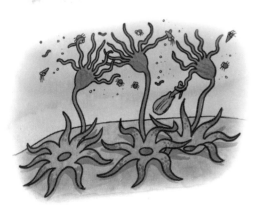

✋ Stalks and tubes

Some animals burrowed into the sea bed for safety. Sea lilies grew long hard stalks to attach themselves to the sea bed, then they waved their feathery arms around to trap food.

? True or false

Prehistoric sea monsters ate jellyfish.

Answer: True
Jellyfish were among the first animals to live in the sea. Later they floated in the ocean with huge fish and sea reptiles and sometimes were eaten!

When were fish as big as buses?

Many early fish had hard bony armor and scales. Some fish were huge, with thick plates like helmets on their heads. Others even had fins covered in bone. The giant fish called *Dunkleosteus* was around 9 meters (30 feet) long, with a head the size of a car. Its jaws were lined by bony plates that were like very, very sharp teeth. *Dunkleosteus* lurked on the sea bed and, when food passed by, snapped its jaws shut to chop the meal in half.

Fish out of water

The prehistoric lungfish used gills to breathe underwater. It also had a kind of airbag-lung called a swim bladder. If the river dried up, the lungfish could breathe air and tunnel into the mud to wait for rain.

8

Which fish crawl along the ocean floor?

Coelacanths use their strong fins to perch or crawl on the ocean floor. Until 1938, when fishermen discovered them in the Indian Ocean, scientists thought coelacanths were no longer around. It was thought that coelacanths had disappeared at the same time as the dinosaurs.

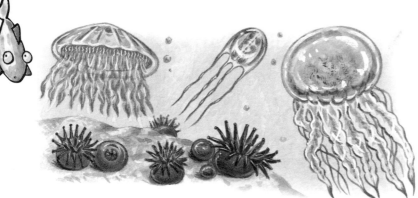

👆 **Stinging attack**

Some animals developed sting cells to defend themselves. They also trapped food in long, whip-like tentacles with sting cells that stung and paralyzed their prey before it was eaten.

Do you know?

1. Fish had backbones and so were the first what?
2. What were prehistoric shark skeletons made from?
3. The first fish were like what with fins?

1. vertebrates. 2. cartilage 3. worms.

Which squirts stick to a rock for life?

Sea squirts live in the ocean. Baby sea squirts have fins and swim around like tadpoles. They also have a flexible rod in the tail, which is like a simple backbone. Young sea squirts soon lose their tails and find a comfortable home on a rock, shell, crab, or boat — and stick to it for life!

9

When were flies as big as seagulls?

Plants first grew on dry land a very long time ago. Insects ate their juicy leaves. Some early insects were much bigger than insects today. From their fossils, we can measure dragonflies with wings as long as a seagull's. These mega-flies zoomed around the swampy forests, catching other insects to eat.

dragonfly

centipede

giant millipede

grasshopper

Ichthyostega

Which water animal first went for a walk?

The first bony animals to crawl out of water onto the land looked like fish with legs and tails. They could breathe air, and they waddled around on stumpy legs. They still swam, like fish, and stayed close to water. These animals, such as *Ichthyostega*, were the first amphibians – animals that can live both on land and in water.

cockroach

giant centipede

👉 Food chain

Plants growing on land were eaten by land animals like worms and insects. Big insects such as dragonflies ate small insects. Amphibians such as the first frogs ate insects. We call this a food chain.

Why were eggshells a great invention?

Amphibians, such as frogs, need to find water to lay their jelly-like eggs. Without water the eggs can dry up and die. One group of animals called reptiles got around this. Creatures like *Hylonomus* laid eggs with a tough rubbery shell, which protected the baby inside from drying out.

Hylonomus

? True or false

Prehistoric trees could catch flies.

Answer: True
Prehistoric pine trees oozed a sticky sap that hardened and became a fossil called amber. Flies trapped in the sap can still be seen inside lumps of amber today.

Which reptiles had enormous radiators?

Keeping not too warm and not too cool can be a problem for animals. Some prehistoric reptiles, such as *Dimetrodon*, kept themselves comfortable with a big sail-fin on their backs that acted like a radiator. If it got cold, they turned sideways to the Sun so that the heat warmed up the sail. When *Dimetrodon* was too hot, it turned its back to the Sun and cooled down by losing heat from its large sail-fin.

Hot and cold blood

Reptiles today are cold-blooded. They need the Sun's warmth to give them energy to move. Warm-blooded animals like mammals make their own energy from food. Dinosaurs, too, may have been warm-blooded.

Did reptiles grow whiskers?

Some reptiles looked more like dogs or pigs than lizards. Some ate plants, chomping tough leaves and digging up roots with their tusk-teeth. Others were hunters, with sharp, biting teeth. These hunting reptiles had whiskers like dogs, which they used as feelers to snuffle their way around.

 Fast and slow movers

Many early reptiles moved slowly on sprawled-out limbs. Others, like crocodiles, lifted their bodies off the ground to crawl. Dinosaurs stood upright and could run.

What can you find in a rock sandwich?

An especially old fossil was found in a quarry in Scotland, squashed between thin layers of rock like the filling in a sandwich. "Lizzie" died a very long time ago. She was 30 centimeters (12 inches) long, with short legs. She lived in a forest of tree ferns near a lake, where spiders, scorpions, and millipedes scuttled around.

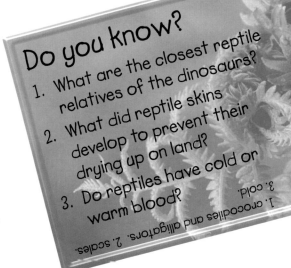

Do you know?
1. What are the closest reptile relatives of the dinosaurs?
2. What did reptile skins develop to prevent their drying up on land?
3. Do reptiles have cold or warm blood?

1. crocodiles and alligators. 2. scales. 3. cold.

Which dinosaur had a thumb on its nose?

In 1822 an English woman named Mary Ann Mantell and her husband Dr. Gideon Mantell found teeth from a dinosaur they named *Iguanodon*. When scientists put *Iguanodon*'s bones together to make a skeleton, they were left with a large claw. Puzzled as to where to put it, they attached it to the dinosaur's nose, like a rhino horn. In fact, *Iguanodon* had two spiky claws – one on each thumb!

Why did dinosaurs get stuck in the mud?

Dinosaur fossils are often found near prehistoric swamps or tar pits. Big animals got stuck in them and died. Meat-eating dinosaurs feeding on the bodies got stuck as well.

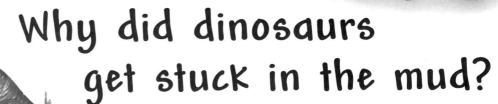

Why did scientists fight over dinosaur bones?

Dinosaur hunting was very popular about 150 years ago, especially in North America. Fossil hunters went out in groups looking for bones. When they found new dinosaurs, scientists often argued over them and gave the same new animal different names.

👆 Plaster casts

When fossils are found, they are removed very carefully. Bones are then wrapped in plaster to protect them. Wet plaster may be poured over delicate remains like this trilobite. When the plaster dries, a hard copy of the trilobite is left.

? True or false

Meat-eating dinosaurs grew new teeth if they lost their old ones.

Answer: True
Meat-eating dinosaurs such as Tyrannosaurus rex often broke a tooth trying to bite the bumpy, leathery bodies of their prey. A new tooth then grew in its place.

Which dinosaurs carried clubs?

A slow, lumbering dinosaur such as *Stegosaurus* could not run faster than a hungry enemy. Instead, it stood still and waved its spiky tail from side to side. Armor-plated dinosaurs such as *Ankylosaurus* did the same. At the end of its tail was a bony club, heavy enough to knock an enemy off its feet. If a giant plant-eater such as *Diplodocus* was in danger, it lashed its long tail like a whip.

Plant-eaters

Plant-eating animals are called herbivores. The sauropods, like *Diplodocus*, did not chew their food. Leaves went down into their vast stomachs, along with stones that they swallowed to help mash up the food.

Diplodocus

Stegosaurus

Which dinosaurs had horn fights?

The fiercest flesh-eaters (carnivores) thought twice about taking on *Triceratops*. This dinosaur had a horn on its nose and two more horns poking out above its eyes. Rival males probably locked horns when fighting each other.

Ankylosaurus

Triceratops

Do you know?

1. What does the name "dinosaur" mean?
2. What do herbivores eat?
3. What do carnivores eat?

1. terrible lizard. 2. plants. 3. meat.

17

Did dinosaur babies go to a nursery?

Fossil hunters have found the nests, eggs, and even babies of dinosaurs. Some dinosaurs laid their eggs by scraping out hollows in sand or soil and burying them. Some laid more than 30 eggs, perhaps in a special "nursery" area with many nests. The small babies were unable to look after themselves, so parent dinosaurs would have been kept busy!

? True or false

Plant-eating dinosaurs were bigger than meat-eaters.

Answer: True
The biggest land animals ever were the plant-eating sauropods, such as Argentinosaurus, which weighed 100 tons. It was ten times heavier than the biggest meat-eating dinosaurs.

👆 **Dinosaur droppings**

Fossilized dinosaur droppings are called coprolites. These look like sausage-shaped pebbles. At one time people thought they were fossil fir cones!

Which dinosaur had the biggest feet?

Dinosaur footprints have been found in ancient rocks, which were soft mud when the dinosaur wandered by. Some plant-eating dinosaurs had very big feet. One of the biggest belonged to a duck-billed dinosaur whose footprint measured 1.36 meters (53½ inches) long – making an elephant look almost dainty!

Maiasaura

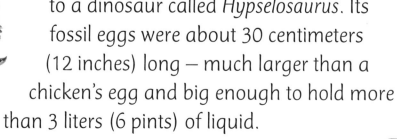

Which dinosaur laid the biggest egg?

Some of the biggest eggs yet found belong to a dinosaur called *Hypselosaurus*. Its fossil eggs were about 30 centimeters (12 inches) long – much larger than a chicken's egg and big enough to hold more than 3 liters (6 pints) of liquid.

19

Which were the first reptiles with wings?

Bigger than any birds, huge flying reptiles soared above prehistoric cliff tops, some swooping down to scoop fish from the waves in their long jaws. Flying reptiles, or pterosaurs, were close relatives of the dinosaurs. They had enormous wings, and some had long tails they used to steady themselves and steer. These bat-like reptiles were probably good gliders and some could flap their wings too.

Which was the biggest animal ever to fly?

A long time ago, a flying reptile as big as a light aircraft took off on the wind. It was called *Quetzalcoatlus*. Its bat-like wings each measured 6 meters (20 feet) across, making it the biggest animal ever to soar into the skies.

Gliding

Warm air currents rise up, and pterosaurs used these to take off and glide into the skies. Air also rises over hillsides and cliffs, where pterosaurs gathered to hunt.

Did early birds bite worms?

The first birds had scaly legs, but they also had something different – feathers. The most famous early bird is *Archaeopteryx*. It looked like a reptile with feathers and was the size of a crow. Its dinosaur-like mouth had teeth, which it used to bite worms or anything else juicy to eat.

Archaeopteryx

Caudipteryx

Fish food

Fossilized fish have been found in some pterosaur tummies. Pterosaurs could fish as they flew. Their long jaws with saw-like teeth snatched slippery fish out of the water.

Do you know?

1. What were the wings of pterosaurs made from?
2. What did *Archaeopteryx* have on its wings and tail?
3. What reptile feature may have developed into bird feathers?

1. skin and long finger. 2. feathers. 3. scales.

Which sea reptile held the long-neck record?

Long-necked sea monsters really did exist during the Age of the Dinosaurs. A sea reptile called *Tanystropheus* had a neck that took up half of its 6-meter (19½-feet) length. Using its neck as a kind of fishing rod, the animal could swing and dip its small head into the sea to snatch fish in its sharp teeth. The longest dinosaur neck was on a land-living sauropod. Its neck was 11 meters (36 feet) long!

Tanystropheus

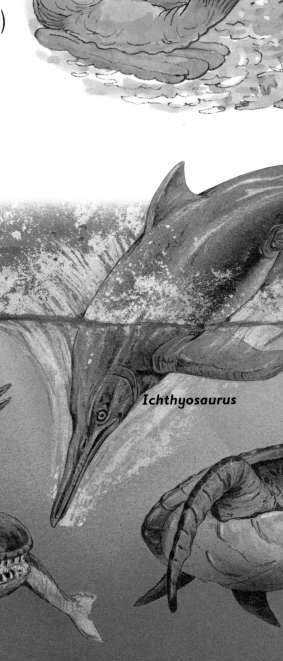

Ichthyosaurus

Taking to the water

Crocodiles first lived on land, but some later took to the sea. Some had paddles instead of feet and grew fins on their tails to help them swim more speedily.

Which sea reptiles leapt above the waves like dolphins?

Ichthyosaurs leapt and darted through warm ocean waves. These speedy reptile swimmers were streamlined and fish-shaped, with big fins, flippers, and flattened tails. They probably swam like dolphins or porpoises, hunting fish, smaller reptiles, and shellfish.

Archelon

Paddling turtles

Giant turtles lived in prehistoric seas, "flying" through the water with their huge front paddles. One called Archelon grew to almost 4 meters (13 feet).

Which dinosaurs were the fiercest fighters?

Most ferocious of the killer dinosaurs was *Tyrannosaurus rex*. It was one of the biggest meat-eaters that ever lived on land. It roamed the forests, waiting to pounce on plant-eating dinosaurs. *Tyrannosaurus rex* was so big that it was safe from any other dinosaurs. Running on strong back legs, it was balanced by its tail. Its small front arms look weak, but the sharp claws and vicious jaws — with 60 sharp-edged teeth — could easily kill!

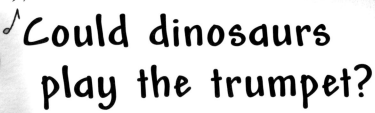

Could dinosaurs play the trumpet?

No, but some dinosaurs may have sounded musical. One had a huge hollow crest on its head, over 1½ meters (5 feet) long, like a horn sticking out backward. When scientists made a model of its skull and blew through it, they heard a noise like a trumpet.

☞ **Dead end for dinosaurs**

Dinosaurs disappeared a very long time ago. Furry mammals, feathered birds, and a few reptiles lived on. But dinosaurs came to a dead end.

Do you know?

1. How big was Compsognathus, the smallest dinosaur?
2. Which animal was king of the dinosaurs?
3. Where did Tyrannosaurus rex live?

1. as big as a chicken. 2. Tyrannosaurus rex. 3. North America.

Could a dinosaur have won a race with a horse?

Racehorses gallop at about 60 kilometers (36 miles) an hour. Some dinosaurs ran faster than this. To find a dinosaur's speed, scientists measure the distance between the footprints it left behind. *Dromiceiomimus* ran on two legs, perhaps as fast as an ostrich — which can reach speeds of up to 65 kilometers (40 miles) an hour.

When did cats have teeth like carving knives?

After the dinosaurs died out, mammals ruled the world. Among the fiercest hunters was the saber-toothed cat. Like a lion without a mane, this animal had two dagger-like teeth. Long, and sharp as carving knives, they stabbed and tore into flesh. Saber-tooths opened their mouths very wide. They probably leapt onto animals such as rhinoceroses, sinking their teeth into the thick skin.

Were mammals alone?

Mammals were not alone. Giant birds stalked the grassy plains and woodlands, hunting for prey. These big birds could not fly. The fierce *Diatryma* looked like a cross between an eagle and an ostrich and stood taller than a human. Such a bird could chase and catch animals with its huge claws and horny, hooked beak.

New grass

When the dinosaurs died out, the Age of the Mammals began. Forests covered much of the Earth but as the climate grew cooler and drier, a new food for plant-eating animals – grass – appeared. Early types of horses, dogs, and cats roamed the grassy plains.

Mammals

Small mammals lived with dinosaurs for many years. They looked like rats and ate insects (and probably dinosaur eggs). Warm-blooded, hairy mammals were active in the cold, unlike reptiles, and gave birth to live young.

? True or false

Some prehistoric lions had pouches like kangaroos.

Answer: True
There were many marsupial mammals that carried their young in pouches. The "marsupial lion" Thylacoleo was the largest marsupial meat-eater of Australia, even though it was only as big as a large dog.

When did elephants play in the snow?

Elephants today live in the hot lands of Africa and Asia. A very long time ago though, some elephants lived in the Ice Age snows. These huge, shaggy mammoths were kept warm by a layer of fat under a yellow wool coat, covered by dark brown hair. Some prehistoric elephants had four tusks and very short trunks. Others had tusks that turned down – useful for digging in the hard soil and ice.

Where is a freezer full of mammoths?

Woolly mammoths lived in Europe and Northern Asia. Deep-frozen mammoths are sometimes dug up, after being buried in ice for thousands of years. Some people have even tried eating thawed mammoth steaks!

When might a dog have looked like a bear?

Hunting on the new grasslands were animals that were half bear and half dog. Among them was *Amphicyon*, which was as big as a grizzly bear. Its head was like a dog's, with bone-crushing teeth. It probably hunted in a pack, like wolves today, eating both plants and meat.

👉 **Tusks for building**

Mammoth tusks are enormously long ivory teeth. Prehistoric people hunted mammoths for food. They used the tusks for tent poles and to make walls for huts in which to shelter from the cold.

Do you know?

1. What did mammoths use to clear snow and reach grass?
2. What kind of animals did giraffes develop from?
3. Which of the big woolly animals had a horn on its snout?

1. tusks. 2. deer. 3. rhinoceros.

Which land mammal was bigger than an elephant?

The land mammal that beat all others for size was a prehistoric rhinoceros called *Baluchitherium*. This heavyweight was bigger than any elephant – even a woolly mammoth! It had no horns, but was eight times heavier than a rhino of today! *Baluchitherium* was 8 meters (26 feet) long and more than 5 meters (16 feet) high – about as tall as a giraffe. It lived in Asia, munching leaves from the treetops.

What kind of animal had a trunk and rhinoceros feet?

A very long time ago, South America was an island. Animals there were different from those in the rest of the world. One looked like a camel without a hump, but its feet were like those of a rhinoceros. Its name was *Macrauchenia*. With its short flexible trunk, it grasped leaves to eat and sniffed the air for danger.

30

Cave artists

Prehistoric people lived in caves during the Ice Age and drew pictures of animals on the cave walls. The pictures, which you can still see today, show horses, deer, wild cattle, and other animals that the cave people hunted for food.

? True or false

Many mammals could fly in prehistoric times.

Answer: False
The only flying mammals are bats. They have been on Earth for about 50 million years. Some of the world's caves have been home to bats since prehistoric times.

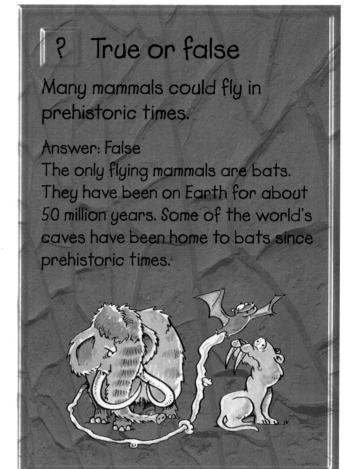

Land bridge

South America stopped being an island when the sea level fell and created a "land bridge" with North America. Mammals in South America then had to fight for food and space with mammals, such as wolves and horses, coming from North America.

31

Index